Save Money &
Build Wealth

The Abundance Plan

Part of 'The Abundance Plan' Book Series

SPIRITUAL PRINCIPLES
OF MONEY

GROWING AND STEWARDING MONEY
GOD'S WAY

By Krista Dunk

100X
PUBLISHING

Spiritual Principles of Money
© 2019 by Krista Dunk
www.SaveMoneyandBuildWealth.com

This title is also available in Kindle format.

Published by 100X Publishing
Vacaville, CA
www.100Xacademy.com

ISBN: 978-1-6919-4182-7

Printed in the United States of America

DEDICATION

This book is dedicated to everyone who feels that there is more to be discovered in God and those who will not settle for anything less than His best.

"And you shall remember the Lord your God,
for it is He who gives you power to get wealth,
that He may establish His covenant which He
swore to your fathers, as it is this day."
—Deuteronomy 8:18

TABLE OF CONTENTS

How to Use This Book

Welcome to *Spiritual Principles of Money*. Before we begin, here are a few thoughts on how to get the most out of reading.

First of all, realize this book will not give you a 100% comprehensive, everything there ever was to know about what God says about money. I'm not sure anyone besides Jesus has the fullness of that revelation. What it *will* give you are pieces of a much larger puzzle – wisdom nuggets I've learned through the years and want to share with you.

Everything God says is meant to shape our perspectives and hearts, leading to up-leveled attitudes and actions. Thinking God's way does not come naturally, whether it be about money, relationships or any other area of life. Our logical minds and selfish nature works against His wisdom, every time. As you read, if you find yourself not understanding or not getting a picture of the principle, it could be one of two issues:

1. You learned something contrary in the past, and your established belief system won't allow you to accept something new (because that would mean you were wrong, and being wrong equals being a failure…which is also not true).

2. You have not yet asked Jesus to be Lord of your life.

When a person comes to believe God is real and that Jesus came to Earth so we could have our personal relationship with God re-established (through Jesus' crucifixion), a transaction in our spirit takes place. The Holy Spirit (just like we are three parts—body, soul, spirit—God has a spirit, too) takes up residence in our spirit. God sent Jesus, and Jesus sent Holy Spirit.

When the Holy Spirit is within us, suddenly what God says—His truths, His ways, His wisdom—jumps off the page and our hearts begin to understand it. It's a beautiful, amazing mystery, and absolutely true. A simple, honest prayer can change everything for you. More on this prayer and topic on page 66.

"But the natural man does not receive the things of the Spirit of God, for they are foolishness to him; nor can he know them, because they are spiritually discerned."
—1 Corinthians 2:14

In *Spiritual Principles of Money*, each short chapter will be a thought, a principle, building on the previous one. As you read through, you'll get new ways to view money and use money. Let these principles ruminate and stew inside your heart and mind. There will be stories and examples. You can jot down some notes and thoughts. Feel free to share your ah-ha moments, ideas, feedback and questions in our Facebook group. Other people may benefit from hearing about your journey.

www.facebook.com/groups/savemoneyandbuildwealth

Here at Save Money and Build Wealth, we are glad you're here. Enjoy reading and learning with us!

Blessings to you,
Krista Dunk (the Money Mindset Maven)
Chris Dunk (the Make Money Master)
Chris Creekpaum (the Save Money Maven)

INTRODUCTION

Did you know that the Bible talks about money more than any other specific topic? Why do you think that is? Why is this topic so important?

Money can become a god. People will serve it. People will worship it. People will follow it wherever it leads. People will go to great lengths for it, even harming others. People will put their trust in it and dependence upon it. However, money doesn't reciprocate the love. Money doesn't love you. Money holds no loyalty to you. Money makes a terrible master.

But we need money, right? So how do we have money—and hopefully a good amount of it—without it ruling over and ruining us?

Money is supposed to be a tool; a tool used to serve you, not vice versa. The Bible is a life-wisdom book, discussing every topic needed to keep our souls healthy. In *Spiritual Principles of Money*, many financial principles will originate from biblical wisdom, or otherwise known as God's Kingdom. Whether you're a Bible-believing person or not, the effectiveness of the wisdom cannot be denied.

God does things differently than people do. As you'll see, sometimes the money principles God has go against traditional, worldly wisdom. For example, how does being generous cause a person to prosper more? If I give away 10% of my income (a tithe), how does God make the 90% that's left do more and go further than keeping 100% would have? It just doesn't seem to be logical that somehow giving away some of your money ends up getting you more.

However, if we recognize the superior, more advanced system of managing and growing money that's based on stewardship, generosity, legacy, blessing, and prosperity, we'll be on a better track. It's a higher level of understanding that is, once again, the best for our souls. Our human logic isn't always trustworthy. Often our human logic is based only on what we've learned and/or what we've experienced. Our knowledge and our experiences are a very limited frame of reference.

"The blessing of the Lord makes one rich, and He adds no sorrow with it." – Proverbs 10:22

Being able to mentor you about money through our Save Money and Build Wealth community cannot be complete without this book and these principles. We'd be doing you a disservice by not introducing you to God's Kingdom system for money, or making it seem like we've had financial success by doing things on our own without God's help.

Managing our money according to His ways has made all the difference, and we cannot stress that fact enough to you.

Each of us has a relationship with money, and we pray your relationship with it will be blessed and healthy. Are you ready?

CHAPTER 1

DAILY BREAD

Inspired by a teaching from Jim Baker's book:
How Heaven Invades Your Finances.

Spiritual Principle: *God promises to provide*
for our basic needs.

"Therefore do not worry, saying, 'What shall we eat?' or
'What shall we drink?' or 'What shall we wear?'
For after all these things the Gentiles seek. For your
heavenly Father knows that you need all these things."
—Matthew 6:31-32

Part of God's promise to us is that He will meet our basic needs each day. The wonderful thing is, there's no striving, works, toil or stress required on our part to "make it happen." He meets our basic needs simply because He loves us. When Jesus taught His disciples how to pray, He included the phrase *give us this day our daily bread*. God knows we need food, water, shelter and clothing. He loves us too much to leave us begging.

"I have been young, and now am old; yet I have not seen
the righteous forsaken, nor his descendants begging bread."
—Psalm 37:25

In the Old Testament, when the Children of Israel wandered the desert for 40 years in search of the Promised Land, God literally fed them with a bread-like substance called manna every morning. God was displeased if people tried to stock up on manna for the next day, showing they didn't really trust in His faithful provision (with the exception of stocking up on the 6th day purposefully to save for the 7th day).

In Pastor Jim's excellent book, *How Heaven Invades Your Finances*, he makes this concept clear. He says a person must have "a basic trust that God will provide for my needs because He loves me. If we don't have this as our initial foundation, any other biblical principles of finance are easily distorted..."

This makes a lot of sense. We are not *earning* our daily bread. We are not having to sow and work tirelessly for our daily bread. It is a gift. A good parent doesn't make their seven-year-old child work and strive for their sandwich.

He goes on to say, "Have you ever seen an anorexic bird? No. Have you seen birds freaking out or having an anxiety attack lately over provision? No. But the Christians sure are. Why are these birds at such peace? What do they know that we need to learn? They have an inner revelation that 'my Father in heaven loves me. Ahhhhh. I can rest. I am going to be okay. And that means I can soar.'"

Look outside. Birds aren't stressed – they're just on the lookout for their provision. Lastly, Pastor Jim shares this thought:

"Sowing and reaping is a correct biblical principle. It is just not supposed to be used to get your needs met."

Does this image change your perspective? Are you able to trust God to meet your basic needs? Do you believe you are special and highly valuable to God? Do you have full faith that He is taking care of you?

God's heart for us is:
- God promises to meet His people's daily needs for provision because He loves us.
- Our daily bread is a gift. We are not earning it.

CHAPTER 2

MONEY IS A TOOL

Spiritual Principle: *Money is an effective tool when in the hands of someone mature.*

I mentioned it once already, and hold on to this valuable thought from now on: <u>money is a tool</u>.

Money is a tool you can use to get a lot accomplished in life. But, it's a tool that can do harm if used improperly. Here's what I mean.

My son is a great kid. I love him so much! But, say that Chris and I had some major yard work to do at our house. Would it be a good idea to give our son a chainsaw and send him out the back door as a 5-year-old? "Here ya go, Buddy, cut away!" Umm, no. Sending a 5-year-old child outside with a substantial power tool would mean we'd be horrible, irresponsible parents. Child Protective Services would certainly be at our doorstep soon thereafter. Chances are *very good* he'd hurt himself, someone else and/or our property with that chainsaw. He couldn't handle it.

But, our son is 18 and strong now. He is well able to use a chainsaw and get some work done outside. Why?

Because he's matured and gained strength. He's proven his responsibility. He's a smart kid. He understands our instruction. He can handle it without it hurting himself, others or our property.

Money can harm people with immature character or lack of skills. We see it all the time in professional sports athletes who suddenly get enormous, multi-million-dollar player contracts. Hollywood stars or entertainers thrust into the limelight often show up on tabloids and news stories with drug arrests, affairs or other destructive lifestyles. It also shows up in the lives of lottery winners. Time Magazine once had a story called "How Winning the Lottery Makes You Miserable." Some statistics say the large lottery windfall will end in 70% of winners going broke just a handful of years later. And sadly, the mega rich are not immune to suicide.

It seems that in some cases, money can amplify a person's character flaws. Money truly cannot buy happiness. Either you're happy or you're not – with or without loads of money.

Money can also harm others when it's in the hands of those with dark motives. You know exactly what I'm talking about. Drug dealers, suicide bombers (and there are even those who pay the bomber's family after the attack), pornography, wire fraud and identity theft, human trafficking, etc. It begs the question, what are we supporting?

In the hands of those with good character, good motives and maturity, money is a tool that can build great, lasting things. Let's pay close attention, being very purposeful about how we use our money tool.

God's heart for us is:
- He wants us to have money when our character is ready to handle it well.

CHAPTER 3

MONEY IS A SEED

Spiritual Principle: *Money works like a seed.*

Did you know that every single time we spend, we are seeding something? It's true. Money is a tool, and it's also a seed. Every time we buy from a store or spend on a service, we are increasing that business or product and the demand for it.

If you buy books, you increase the amount of books that are written. If we spend at coffee shops, more coffee shops will open. When money is spent on horror movies, the number of horror movies filmed increases. When a person spends on immoral things, immorality increases. That's how it works. Our money is a seed that increases whatever it's sown into. Money seed does what it does: it grows and increases stuff, whether it's detrimental or beneficial. What we spend on matters…a lot.

By purchasing this book (and possibly the whole Abundance Plan set), you are increasing learning; your learning and others'. You have seeded and increased your knowledge. It also helps us and increases our ability to continue creating more content, tips and strategies for people.

My friend, Pedro Adao, runs an amazing group for Kingdom business owners/entrepreneurs called 100X Academy. In one of his trainings, he introduced this biblical money principle:

As Kingdom people, we save to sow.

The world may save to accumulate, but we save in order to sow into good soil. Good soil could be sowing our tithes and offerings to churches and ministries. It may be supporting missionaries or going on mission trips ourselves. However, sowing with money includes many other things like getting counseling and spiritual mentoring so your heart can be healed of past hurts, purchasing a piece of equipment for your business to expand, purchasing an investment property, enrolling in a class so you can increase your knowledge and skills, developing an orchard, buying stock of a company you support, helping to pay for the education of a student, hiring a coach, etc. These are examples of sowing in good soil, too.

*"But he who received seed **on the good ground** is he who hears the word and understands it, who indeed bears fruit and produces: some a hundredfold, some sixty, some thirty."*
— Matthew 13:23

To have the hundredfold harvest/return Jesus talks about in Matthew 13, Pedro offered these steps:

1. Find good soil.
2. Sow as much as you can.
3. Sow as fast as you can.

Although Jesus was referring to God's Word being sown into the hearts of people, and the soil is our heart's environment, good soil is the key required for every single type of sowing (natural and spiritual) to be successful. Sow into the Kingdom, into yourself and into others. Grow more good. And remember, **you are good soil**.

God's heart for us is:
- He wants us to have money when more good will spread in the world because of what we sow into. Money in the hands of good people spreads more good.
- Be good soil and find good soil. Invest into making your own heart soil better, and invest into good-soil opportunities where God is working.

CHAPTER 4

WHY DO I WANT MONEY?

Spiritual Principle: *God cares about why we want money.*

Why we want money is the real question. Does this question seem silly? *Why do I want money? Doesn't everyone want money?!* Yes, I suppose so, but our deepest motives are key.

Our society, advertisers, movies, TV programs, magazines, social media, and nearly every image flashing by our faces continually screams a version of this thought:

You aren't happy, good enough, thin enough, or valuable enough without having this ___ or looking like this ___.

Masters of manipulation, advertisers and Hollywood sell us lies to get our money. All of the manipulation can produce impulses of greed and low self-images. It's sickening how much of our lives are infiltrated with worthless pursuits, worthless thoughts and worthless feelings because we chase after an image of something not real.

It makes me think of beer commercials. Oh the ridiculousness...for one thing, hardly any women I know actually like beer! Yet every commercial shows (often) scantily clad, very attractive younger women who are smiling, laughing, flirting, dancing, or maybe jumping into a pool or running on a beach, with beer in hand. Everyone is seemingly having the best time of their lives, partying with all their very best friends. *Right*...I'm saying sarcastically.

That's not how it really is at parties with alcohol consumption. Sometimes it looks more like this: Bob starts a fight with Tim, who he doesn't know at all. Kelly and John yell at each other in an irrational, drunken rage. Rick gets a DUI ticket on his way home, when he shouldn't have been driving. Sara spends three hours throwing up and wishing she'd just stayed home. Betty passes out and suspects she was sexually violated the next morning when she wakes up on a stranger's couch. Everyone wonders why it wasn't as fulfilling like the commercials and movies show. So they keep at it, hoping to find acceptance and happiness somehow next time...

Greed, materialism and selfish motives are serious heart problems, although are commonplace in our society. Many people chase money, stuff and status for all the wrong reasons and to the detriment of their own souls. God does not want that for us. Money should be the byproduct of bringing massive value to the lives of others, our communities, employers, customers, clients, etc. If you're dedicated to doing the right thing, helping, working hard, being creative, being responsible, loving well, and continuing to grow and learn, money will start to find you.

"And you shall remember the Lord your God, for it is He who gives you power to get wealth, that He may establish His covenant which He swore to your fathers, as it is this day." –Deuteronomy 8:18

God gives us power to get wealth. That's how the blessing comes. Obedience, wisdom, His direction, He is the source, trust God, sowing and reaping, generosity. We want His blessings, yes? Not for selfish purposes, although to take care of your household, certainly. Put on your own oxygen mask first, then assist others. But, we want to be blessed ourselves to also be a blessing to others.

Here's what we can do today. Stop thinking money will solve all your problems. Stop thinking you have to buy a massive amount of stuff to be happy. Stop thinking your image is priority number one. Stop thinking you have to run ragged after money, no matter what else it costs you. You can always get more money, but broken relationships and reputations are hard to mend and you cannot ever recover lost time.

Get some new thoughts. Happy is attractive. Healthy is attractive. Debt-free is attractive. Kind is attractive. Joy is attractive. Peace is attractive. Honest is attractive.

> *"A wise man should have money in his head,*
> *but not in his heart."* –Jonathan Swift

God's heart for us is:
- He wants us to have pure motives when it comes to money.

CHAPTER 5

THE FIVE USES OF MONEY

Spiritual Principle: *money has specific purposes.*

If you think about it, we really don't need money at all. Money itself is just odd-looking paper or cyberspace numbers on an online bank account screen. What we truly need are the things money is traded for, like food, buying a vehicle, an oven, a coat, clean water, school books, or a new filling at the dentist.

So, when money comes into our lives, some of it is supposed to be consumed (bread) and some is to be sown (seed). Here are the five uses for money:

1. Giving
2. Saving
3. Spending
4. Investing
5. Enjoying

These five uses can be split into three categories:

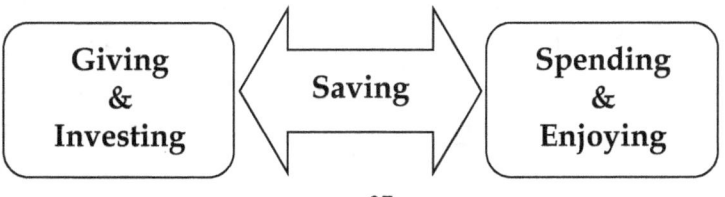

Let's talk about this a bit more. Giving and investing are both examples of sowing. I just want to introduce the idea of how generosity is an investment now, but we'll discuss it more in chapter 12. Investing is the process of putting money into an asset or resource in hopes of growth and a good future return. If you've read *Make Your Money Work for You*, you already know of many ideas for wisely investing money. When you invest, sow and give, that money is not gone forever. It is growing, and you will see gain and increase come back in the future. As you can see in this next statement Jesus makes, sowing into the Kingdom through giving also has a good return.

"Give, and it will be given to you: good measure, pressed down, shaken together, and running over will be put into your bosom. For with the same measure that you use, it will be measured back to you." —Luke 6:38

Spending and enjoying are examples of how money is consumed. It is okay that some of our money is consumed. It's necessary, and it's one of the purposes of why we have it. When we spend on necessary needs like utility bills, a doctor visit, groceries, gas, school fees, insurance or rent, that money is gone...never to be seen again. The same is true for money we spend on "enjoying." What do I mean by that? Enjoyment, fun, travel, gifts, entertainment, an upgraded car, a kiddie swimming pool for the yard, a cool watch, a cold lemonade on a hot day, a hot chocolate on a cold day, and that new shirt because it's your favorite color.

Having the opportunity to use money to enjoy life is good. God really does want us to enjoy life and His blessings. It's also one of the purposes for having money.

"As for every man to whom God has given riches and wealth, and given him power to eat of it, to receive his heritage and rejoice in his labor – this is the gift of God."
—Ecclesiastes 5:19

Saving is in a flexible, middle category of its own. It could go either way, e.g., money that is saved could eventually become money that's consumed or be money that's sown.

The wisest use of money is to use it in this order:

1. **Giving** – tithe to a church, charity, help a friend
2. **Saving** – money into a savings account
3. **Spending** – paying bills and necessary expenses
4. **Investing** – putting money into assets and funds
5. **Enjoying** – frills, extras, entertainment, travel, stuff

Unfortunately, things go wrong and people get into financial trouble when this order is swapped. There are many people whose money use looks more like this:

1. Spending
2. Enjoying
(notice the other three are totally absent...)

These are the instances when credit card and other debts take over and people with fairly good-paying jobs live paycheck to paycheck. If any of these five uses are missing completely, money's full purpose in your life will not be complete and problems will be present.

So, why is giving number one, you may ask? Two reasons: first, people tend to be selfish and greed can creep into our hearts and minds. Giving keeps our hearts right. Second, God says to give the first portion to His house. His Kingdom purposes are always good and worth supporting.

"Bring all the tithes into the storehouse, That there may be food in My house, And try Me now in this," Says the Lord of hosts, "If I will not open for you the windows of heaven And pour out for you such blessing That there will not be room enough to receive it." —Malachi 3:10

God's heart for us is:
- Money has specific uses/purposes and should be used in a particular order.
- Some of our money is bread (to be consumed) and some is seed (to be planted/invested for growth).

CHAPTER 6

INCREASE

Spiritual Principle: *God cares about increase.*

How do I know this is true?

In the Bible, Jesus tells a story called the Parable of the Talents. You can read the whole story in Matthew chapter 25. Maybe you know the story already, but let me summarize. The master of some kind of estate goes away on a long trip. Before he leaves, the master gathers his three servants and gives them each varying amounts of money: 5 talents, 2 talents and 1 talent. From what I once learned, a "talent" would have been worth about $3000 today (some have even said it would be more like $30K).

"For the kingdom of heaven is like a man traveling to a far country, who called his own servants and delivered his goods to them. And to one he gave five talents, to another two, and to another one, to each according to his own ability; and immediately he went on a journey." – Matthew 25:14-15

Amazingly, the first and second servants both double the money the master entrusted them with. We don't know exactly how, but it says they "went and traded with them" (traded with the money). They did some kind of business with it. They used it to create more. When the master came back home from his long journey, those two servants were praised and rewarded. Paraphrasing, the master said, "Well done and nice job good and faithful servants! Since you have shown yourselves faithful with this small task, I'm going to put you in charge of many important things. You bring me joy!"

However, the third servant who received one talent went outside, dug a hole and stuffed the money in it. When the master returned, it didn't go so well for him.

"But his lord answered and said to him, 'You wicked and lazy servant, you knew that I reap where I have not sown, and gather where I have not scattered seed. So you ought to have deposited my money with the bankers, and at my coming I would have received back my own with interest. So take the talent from him, and give it to him who has ten talents.

'For to everyone who has, more will be given, and he will have abundance; but from him who does not have, even what he has will be taken away. And cast the unprofitable servant into the outer darkness. There will be weeping and gnashing of teeth.'" – Matthew 25:26-30

Yikes. Goodbye, unprofitable servant. At the very, *very* least the master was looking for some bank interest! At least that would have been *something*. That was the very least the third servant could have done to satisfy the master's desire for increase. But he didn't do even that. That servant was called wicked and unprofitable.

If there's one thing that jumps out at me from that story, is how important increase is to the master. In this story, the master of the estate is actually a representation of *the Master*, God, and we are the servants entrusted with His goods.

Good stewardship and increase are important to the Master. He puts resources into our hands and expects us to grow them and manage them well. He gives us the seeds and seeds are meant to be planted. The Master would say to us, "I have given you the seeds. Go and plant and produce more." I don't think anyone gives away seeds without the expectation that they will be planted.

Jesus is excellent at telling deep stories with spiritual significance and principles by using simple stories and everyday examples. I hope you can see a mental picture of how important increase is. Whether you have a little or a lot, the principle still applies.

About six years into our marriage, Chris and I were at a point along our financial path when we were finally out of debt (other than our house mortgage) and we had some money saved in the bank. We had no idea what to do with that money! Growing up, neither of us saw any kind of strategies for growing wealth. Thankfully, we did learn that saving was important, and at least we had our money on deposit earning a little bit of interest at the bank. But, somehow inside we knew there had to be much better ways to steward/manage the money. Rich people knew something we didn't. They had strategies we didn't know about for increase. *Now that we have some money, what do we do with it?* We wondered.

The financial gurus and small group curriculums that came around didn't help us much. Most of them were all about getting out of debt and making a budget. Check those two off the list...but what next? We had insurance through our jobs. Check. We had retirement plans moving along through our jobs. Check. It was frustrating, but then we found some mentors! Our learning curve was partially about learning advanced strategies and partially about getting a new money mindset. We had to think differently, and then take action on the new thinking.

For more teaching about getting a new and improved money mindset, read our other book in The Abundance Plan series called *Make Your Money Work for You: Level Up Your Finances with New Mindsets, Planning, Habits and Goals.* But back to the topic of increase, that's what we wanted for our personal finances. And that's what the Master is looking for also.

He is actually looking, right now, for people who are trustworthy with what they have today and who know how to produce more. He's on the lookout for people and families who He can bless.

God's heart for us is:
- He wants those of us who are trustworthy and know how to increase what He's put in our hands to have more.

CHAPTER 7

BLESSING

Spiritual Principle: *God wants to bless His people.*

At the core of the word bless (or blessing), there are two important meanings we should consider. To bless means:

1. To convey something of value.
2. To cause an increase of something that's good.

Have you ever had someone who has blessed you in some way? Did they do something that blessed you? Did they give you something? An item, a gift, a kind word, helped you with a task, prayed for you, paid for something for you, etc.? They conveyed something of value to you. God blesses us in this way, too. He has given us gifts, opportunities, relationships, houses, money, and many more things.

"The Lord has blessed my master greatly, and he has become great; and He has given him flocks and herds, silver and gold, male and female servants, and camels and donkeys."
—Genesis 24:35

And then there's another aspect of "blessing": to place a supernatural command of increase and good upon something or someone. Things can be blessed and people can be blessed. Maybe you've heard someone say something like, "They sent him away with a blessing," or, "They blessed her ministry."

"By faith Jacob, when he was dying, blessed each of the sons of Joseph, and worshiped, leaning on the top of his staff."
— Hebrews 11:21

"And they blessed Rebekah and said to her: 'Our sister, may you become the mother of thousands of ten thousands; And may your descendants possess the gates of those who hate them.'" — Genesis 24:60

A blessing is a thing (a noun) or blessing is also a command or impartation (verb). To pray a prayer of blessing for someone is an action; to lay hands on them and command good towards them – for increase, safety, provision, favor, love, wisdom, etc. It paints a blessing target on someone for their future. It commands and decrees an increase of good for them.

In this section, my main goal is for you to see that God is good and He desires to bless you in both aspects. He has good plans for you. He sees your highest potential. Not only does He love you very much, but He *is* love. When you're good like God is, blessing others (especially your own children) is just a natural outflow of who you are. This is God.

"His divine power has given to us all things that pertain to life and godliness." — 2 Peter 1:3a

"And my God shall supply all your need according to His riches in glory by Christ Jesus." — Philippians 4:19

I want to cite this verse one more time:

"The blessing of the Lord makes one rich, and He adds no sorrow with it." — Proverbs 10:22

Good fathers want to bless their children with as much blessing as they can handle at any given time, taking into consideration their capacity and trustworthiness. God will not give us more (good things) than we can handle. How much blessing are you ready for? How much blessing can you steward well right now?

God's heart for us is:
- He is a good dad who desires to bless His kids and knows how much blessing we can handle well right now.

CHAPTER 8

TRUSTWORTHY

Spiritual Principle: *People who are trustworthy get more resources put into their hands.*

We've experienced this spiritual money principle to be true. In the 26 years we've been married so far, we've gone through a large financial transformation. From starting out with pretty good jobs (for people our ages), getting ourselves into debt and not caring at all about God's money principles, our financial situation is much different now. Although we're constantly still learning, we feel truly abundant now and have more than enough. We lack for nothing.

Something switched when we were in our mid-twenties (thankfully...). I grew up in church, but hadn't attended since I was about 13 years old. At age 20 (me) and 22 (Chris), we married and were very responsible despite our young ages, mostly. Being good stewards of money and building wealth wasn't on our radar then, but at least we succeeded in faithfully pay all our many bills each month.

A couple years later, I started attending church again with my parents when Chris had to work his retail job on the weekends. Soon after, I made the decision to re-dedicate my life to God and doing things His way. Chris wanted nothing to do with it for a while. But he started becoming curious about this *God thing*. He chose to accept Jesus as his Savior after praying with my step-dad one evening. It was a major turning point for us!

Our priorities shifted. It was no longer all about living for ourselves anymore. There were new purposes bigger than ourselves that became more important. Unfortunately debt kept us from being generous in ways we wished we could be. Debt would also keep me at a 40-hour per week job instead of being able to stay home with children we hoped to have some day. It started to feel like a plague.

After discussions, planning, budgeting and putting our plans into action, we paid off every car loan, furniture loan and every credit card. It felt amazing! Before our hearts and checkbooks turned a new leaf, we were not fully trustworthy targets for God's blessing and abundance when it came to money. But now, things were changing.

It was a process of change and new habits, of new thoughts and motives. It didn't happen overnight. Motives, intents of the heart, maturity, obedience, faithfulness are a big deal to God. Every part of our lives should glorify God.

"...thank God for Jesus – now the Gentiles are grafted into the promises of God..." —Sid Roth

I love to watch a show called *It's Supernatural*. The host of the show, Sid Roth, is a Jewish American who has been interviewing pastors, evangelists, prophets, ministers and many others for several decades about their experiences with God and His Kingdom. Sid also travels around the world to teach Jewish communities about Jesus and God's supernatural power. By the way, Gentiles are people of the world who are not Jewish, who are not descended from Abraham and the 12 Tribes of Israel.

In a recent letter he mailed out to viewers, Sid talked about a great wealth transfer that's coming. Here's what he wrote:

> Isaiah says something about Israel that sounds outrageous – especially since most nations in the United Nations hate the Jew and Israel. *"Your eyes will shine, and your heart will thrill with joy, for merchants from around the world will come to you [Israel]. They will bring you the wealth of many lands."* Isaiah 60:5. What will cause this great wealth transfer? It's as Paul says: *"Now if the Gentiles were enriched because the people of Israel turned down God's offer of salvation, think how much greater a blessing the world will share when they*

finally accept it." Romans 11:12. In other words, if in unbelief the Jewish people blessed the world, how much greater blessing will they be to the world in their belief?

People will begin to recognize the great favor God has given to His people, and they'll be compelled to pour into them financially. If we don't know or acknowledge God's heart for Israel, we're missing something...big. In fact, in Psalm 122, the Bible says those who bless Israel will be blessed. *"Pray for the peace of Jerusalem: they that love thee shall prosper."* My point is, God can trust us when we care about and love the things He loves.

Are we trustworthy for great blessing? Will we choose to and do we know how to steward money properly? Just like the story of my son and the chainsaw, can we handle that tool yet? God loves giving more to those who can increase and who are obedient to His plans and purposes.

God's heart for us is:
- He wants us to have money when we understand money itself is not what we should put our trust in. God wants us to trust in and look to Him as our source. He gives us the power to get wealth.
- There is a wealth transfer coming to trustworthy people who love what He loves.

CHAPTER 9

STEWARDSHIP

Spiritual principle: *If the King owns everything, we manage the territory and resources He's placed in our hands.*

Remember the master in the Parable of the Talents? The master owned everything. The master gave the opportunities to his servants. The master also gave rewards (and one punishment) to servants based on their stewardship. To steward means to manage the goods, resources, land, possessions, etc., for the true owner of those items. The steward doesn't own them, but is in charge of managing them. Stewards are like a property or estate manager.

Let's make this concept really clear. Another spot in Jim Baker's book says this: "God is the owner. I am a steward. God has entrusted me with some stuff. It's not my stuff. Somebody had it before me; somebody else will get it after me."

"But who am I, and who are my people, that we could give anything to you? Everything we have has come from you, and we give you only what you first gave us!"
—1 Chronicles 29:14

Every one of us have things we steward: children, relationships, jobs, time, homes, vehicles, and even our physical bodies. We also manage the money we earn. Whether it's an earthly master or a heavenly one, people with assets and great wealth recognize the extreme importance of putting great managers in charge. Selfish managers will serve themselves at the expense of others. Lazy managers will frustrate you. Deceptive managers will cheat you.

> *"And the Lord said, 'Who then is that faithful and wise steward, whom his master will make ruler over his household, to give them their portion of food in due season? Blessed is that servant whom his master will find so doing when he comes. Truly, I say to you that he will make him ruler over all that he has.'"* —Luke 12:42-44

God has an abundance of resources; limitless resources. When He offers some of it for us to take care of, stewardship can become a test of our character and habits. As stewards, we answer to the King, and the King has great blessing in store for good stewards. What's under the care of a good steward multiplies.

God's heart for us is:
- God wants us to have more money when we're wise, faithful stewards of what we have now.

CHAPTER 10

ABUNDANCE

Spiritual principle: *The overflow is for others.*

"And my God shall supply all your need according to His riches in glory by Christ Jesus." — Philippians 4:19

Let's talk about the Rich Fool. In Luke 12, Jesus teaches about him, that he laid up treasure for himself and was not rich towards God. In other words, God gave him the power to get wealth and increase, but he used it improperly. So, what did God expect from this land owner? Here's the story:

"The ground of a certain rich man yielded plentifully. And he thought within himself, saying, 'What shall I do, since I have no room to store my crops?' So he said, 'I will do this: I will pull down my barns and build greater, and there I will store all my crops and my goods. And I will say to my soul, "Soul, you have many goods laid up for many years; take your ease; eat, drink, and be merry."' But God said to him, 'Fool! This night your soul will be required of you; then whose will those things be which you have provided?' "So is he who lays up treasure for himself, and is not rich toward God." — Luke 12:16-21

I believe God's expectation was a combination of things. In this time period (and even sometimes today), crops, livestock and other earthly resources and minerals were traded like money. In essence, they were money. He expected the landowner to have a different mindset about money, but we can see by his example, not every rich person's mindset is proper. Greed took over the Rich Fool's decision-making. He may have thought, "This is it! I have arrived. Now I can retire and live for myself."

Maybe God caused the large crop increase that year to feed that man's community. Maybe God wasn't even asking this landowner to give crops away *free*. Maybe God would have even been pleased if the man had sold some of the abundance he didn't personally need!

> *"The people will curse him who withholds grain, but*
> *blessing will be on the head of him who sells it."*
> —Proverbs 11:26

The Rich Fool instead decided to keep it all for himself and build a bigger barn to store it. That was wrong. Why? **The overflow is for others.** God causes our increase and He has a good, important purpose for it. Sure, the increase also blesses us as it comes in, too.

For the Rich Fool, his unusually large harvest was all about him. Let's not make the same mistake. Instead, let's consider abundance. God has more than enough to supply all our needs. He is the God of limitless supply. Heaven has no lack whatsoever. Don't be the hoarding 6-year-old who can't bring themselves to share a bite of their cake when there's a gigantic-sized extra cake in the refrigerator (plus five more cake mixes in the pantry). Our tendencies towards scarcity and lack thinking will cause us to scrape and scrimp to get ahead, but will fall short. We won't go without when we know God is able to supply all our needs according to His riches, resources, strategies, network, etc.

Abundance is available to us. There is enough. Abundance can come to you. Be trustworthy to be able to handle abundance, proven first by being trustworthy in the small times. Abundance is more than money. True riches has a lot to do with a deep relationship with God, our attitudes, gratefulness, wisdom, and right priorities. Full, abundant life is rich in relationships, finances, health, work, peace, and joy, and it is rich towards God – honoring Him and loving others well. His plan and doing it His way will always be better than ours.

"I have come that they may have life, and that they may have it more abundantly." —Jesus, in John 10:10b

In my friend Josh Kachadorian's book called *Jesus Is…*, he studied the meaning of the word 'abundantly' in this verse. Here's what he discovered:

"The word abundant here refers to *more than we would expect or anticipate, a life that offers us advantage* and *more than what is necessary*." That definition is powerful! And so is this thought: **superabundance**.

Here's one more interesting thought about abundance coming to us in our lives:

> *"Now to Him who is able to do exceedingly abundantly above all that we ask or think, according to the power that works in us, to Him be glory in the church by Christ Jesus to all generations, forever and ever. Amen."*
> —Ephesians 3:20-21

If we know God is our source of abundance (He is from whom all blessings flow), what have we asked Him for? What are we thinking about? Imagine…if His ability to do exceedingly abundant, magnificent things in our lives was based solely on what we're asking of Him and on our thoughts, how would that turn out for us?

God's heart for us is:
- He wants us to have money when it can flow to us…and then through us.
- He wants our whole lives to be abundant, full of good things.

CHAPTER 11

OUTFLOW

Spiritual principle: *The outflow is also beautiful.*

About a two-minute drive or a seven-minute walk from my house, down the hill and around the corner, there is a small stream. This stream is on both sides of the road, flowing underneath through large conduit pipes from one side to the other. Every time we drive by, we take a peek. Sometimes we take a stroll to stand and look at it for a few minutes.

One day, I realized I kept looking only at the side of the stream flowing towards me, rarely gazing at the side flowing away. The Holy Spirit instantly showed me something. We typically focus on God's blessing coming to us, flowing to us, and the glory of that and the desire for that. On the other hand, we miss the equal beauty of what flows away from us and on to others.

"If anyone thirsts, let him come to Me and drink. He who believes in Me, as the Scripture has said, out of his heart will flow rivers of living water." —John 7:37-38

When Jesus spoke of rivers of living water flowing out

49

of a person who believes in Him, this living water must first flow into the person. The source of the water comes, fills them up to capacity, then outflows. So, how does this relate to money?

When we get a financial windfall or blessing we are thrilled, wouldn't you agree? However, sometimes we hold the blessings we've received with tight fists. The flow to us is fantastic, but the thought of blessings (or money) flowing out away from us isn't always as exciting. Sometimes it's terrifying.

But, we need to catch the picture of the river. The river of blessing is as beautiful coming towards us as it is flowing away. And, the bigger the river, the better in this case. Let me share one more personal story.

A while back, I was at a conference where a woman was talking about money. As she walked and talked, she held up a $50 bill. Towards the end of her point, she asked the room, "Who wants this money?" She had to repeat it, as most of us thought she was being rhetorical, but her intent was to give it away. My instant thought was *no, let someone else have it. I don't need it. I'm doing just fine. We have enough.* The Holy Spirit's instant thought right back was *sure, you are doing well and you have enough for yourselves. But what about for others?*

It quickly changed my perspective on why continuing to build wealth is one of the most unselfish things we can do. If I decide I've accumulated enough for my own family's purposes and then rest on my laurels from that point forward, I become the rich fool.

Or, if I believe I have enough and God doesn't want me to have too much, causing me to reject making money, this is also flawed, faulty thinking. In that case, where is the outflow we're supposed to have? A small, trickling brook won't outflow much. A large, raging river's outflow, however, will be vast, affecting much land for miles and miles.

Rather than becoming rich jerks who hoard it all or becoming religious jerks who think reaching for more is somehow a pursuit God does not want for us, let's grab hold of the picture of the beautiful river flowing to us and the beauty of some of it flowing away. A shift inside us will happen.

God's heart for us is:
- When He blesses us, we get filled up first.
- He wants us to have hearts that deeply understand that we've freely received and can freely give.

CHAPTER 12

GENEROSITY

Spiritual principle: *Generosity is an investment.*

"We make a living by what we get. We make a life by what we give." — Winston Churchill

To go along with the thought that our outflow is beautiful, a person who truly understands how powerful generosity is, could say this:

God, I recognize You as my source of provision. You give me the power to get wealth. I choose to be generous because You've chosen to be generous to me. Generosity helps my heart and motives stay clean and good. By being generous and letting the abundance and overflow help others, I'm saying thank you, and I recognize Your authority.

"He who sows sparingly will also reap sparingly, and he who sows bountifully will also reap bountifully. So let each one give as he purposes in his heart, not grudgingly or of necessity; for God loves a cheerful giver."
— 2 Corinthians 9:6-7

Generosity can become a lifestyle. It can be learned and

needs to be, as it doesn't come naturally to us as humans. Part of generosity is tithing. A tithe means a tenth (10%). Many churches encourage their members to give 10% of their income to support the church's work. The concept of tithing was first mentioned in the Bible, way back in Genesis. Jacob, an heir of a man named Isaac and soon to be very prosperous, made this promise to God: "...all that You give me I will surely give a tenth to You."

"Will a man rob God? Yet you have robbed Me!
But you say, 'In what way have we robbed You?'
In tithes and offerings. You are cursed with a curse,
For you have robbed Me, even this whole nation.
Bring all the tithes into the storehouse,
That there may be food in My house,
And try Me now in this," Says the Lord of hosts,
"If I will not open for you the windows of heaven
And pour out for you such blessing
That there will not be room enough to receive it.
"And I will rebuke the devourer for your sakes,
So that he will not destroy the fruit of your ground,
Nor shall the vine fail to bear fruit for you in the field,"
Says the Lord of hosts..." —Malachi 3:8-11

God owns everything and is the source of all provision, but asks for 10% back. By giving, we remind ourselves of where our help comes from. It's like He bought a pizza and gave the whole thing to me. The pizza was cut into ten pieces, and He asked to have one piece for Himself after giving it to me. Even though He brought it, I still have the choice to say, "No, You can't have one." Chances are, He may not bring me more pizza in that case!

In the verse from Malachi above, God Himself says the 10% is sacred. By us keeping it, He considers it robbery. Strong words! It's meant to be resources used to accomplish His purposes. Withholding what He considers sacred withholds His favor.

Favor: to have special privileges, opportunities and to be preferred above others based on a relationship with someone in a high-ranking, decision-making, door-opening position.

But, by honoring this principle there is an enormous promise of blessing. A blessing is literally built into giving. God promises to pour out a blessing upon us so large we won't be able to contain it all. Plus, anything that may try to devour our wealth will be rebuked (cut off/stopped/diverted).

Interestingly, mainstream financial advisors often recommend 10% as the perfect portion of your income to donate/give to charitable causes. Gee, I wonder where they got that idea from!

At its most basic level, the word investment means

putting a resource into (vesting in) something and expecting whatever resource was invested to increase. Put in a certain amount, get more back in return. In fact ROI stands for Return on Investment. We can invest into God's plans.

I believe when we invest in things God cares about and supports, somehow that giving makes 90% become more than 100%. Sure our 10% may leave our account, but somehow a special blessing gets put upon the remaining 90%. Our pastor has a saying:

"Put God in your budget."

He also likes to say, "You can't out give God." I don't know exactly how God does it, but I've seen generosity and giving produce results time and time again. It may come in the form of a special opportunity. It may be an unexpected raise. A refund comes. A promotion, an inheritance, a special deal or discount comes up, something of yours that wasn't selling suddenly sells, someone gives you something for free, or any number of miraculous circumstances happen just in time.

Chris and I are dedicated tithers to our church. Our church helps our community in many ways. Several years ago, we sold a home we had lived in for ten years and we were searching for vacant land to build on. My sister's husband came across a piece of land they wanted to buy and a vacant parcel was next door...*not for sale*. After finally locating the owner, we asked if he'd consider selling it to us. He said no, he was saving it to give to his kids someday. But, when he heard it was two sisters wanting their families to live next door to each other, he changed his mind! We bought the property (and so did my sister's family) and started making plans to build.

In our area, building comes with many rules, regulations and restrictions. Nearly every property in an area like ours has to have environmental studies and even tests to determine the presence of certain protected animal species. It's a burdensome, long process. When our builder checked our parcels' records at the county office, he learned our properties were grandfathered into *not* needing any studies at all if we broke ground within the next three months. There was a ten-year window for this policy to apply to us and our two lots, and we hit it in the nick of time. To us, this whole situation was a miracle. God worked it out on our behalf.

No one could ever convince me otherwise – generosity has many benefits. It's a blessing for you, for others and gets God's good work done. Win-win-win!

"Give, and it will be given to you: good measure, pressed down, shaken together, and running over will be put into

your bosom. For with the same measure that you use, it will be measured back to you." —Luke 6:38

Here is a thought inspired by Pastor Dave Minton: God will always resource what (who) takes care of His Kingdom. When we are in His will and when we get blessed, God gets the glory and we eat the fruit. He gets the glory for providing the blessings, for His marvelous power and for His faithfulness, and we get to enjoy the blessing.

God's heart for us:
- God wants us to have money so we can have many opportunities to be generous.
- Generosity is a Kingdom characteristic.

CHAPTER 13

GROW, CREATE, BUILD

Spiritual Principle: *The Kingdom is about growth, God is the Creative Force, and He calls us to help build.*

However you say it — grow, create or build — they all equal increase and expansion.

Just as we grow spiritually and the Kingdom's influence is supposed to grow, we can grow wealth by putting it into good soil; good investments that produce a harvest over time.

Just as God is the Creator and He has made us creative like Him, we can create wealth by using our gifts, skills, talents, abilities, and creative ideas to open up entirely new streams of income for our family.

Just as God is called the Master Builder and He also calls us to rise up and build, we can build wealth by starting businesses, buying real estate, inventing, investing, and other ventures that allow us to build and carry forward income and returns.

We can build businesses, build people up (through kindness, teaching, love, mentoring, etc.), create art, music and services that bless people, create blueprints, buildings and environments where people can rest and heal, grow healthy food to nourish bodies, and even grow wealth. All of these things are pleasing to God, when done with the right heart motives. Every single thing we do with pure, loving motives that brings more good and light into the world pleases God, including making money.

Expansion, increase, growth, creating and building – all of it is about making a meaningful difference in the world. When you become a good steward (manager) of your finances, yes it benefits you and your family first. But it should also move out beyond your borders to impact and bless other families, the causes you support, churches, non-profits, schools, etc. Because remember, the overflow of our abundance is for others.

I've heard a lot about the "Law of Attraction" and how we supposedly can attract money. I don't know about all that, but I do for sure know that when we bring massive value to the lives of others and help support God's plans on the earth, money will flow to us. When we add value, something of value comes back.

When we act like God—creators, builders and growers of good things—we live our best life, we are blessed and so are others.

"And I told them of the hand of my God which had been good upon me, and also of the king's words that he had spoken to me. So they said, 'Let us rise up and build.' Then they set their hands to this good work."
— Nehemiah 2:18

God's heart for us is:
- God made us in His image – creative builders who are meant to grow and expand what He's entrusted us with.
- God is pleased with His people making money.

CHAPTER 14

WEALTH AND RICHES

Inspired by a teaching from Keith Ferrante, prophet and pastor. Learn more at emergingprophets.com.

Spiritual Principle: *Wealth is an inheritance; riches are accumulated.*

The Parable of the Talents (and also the Parable of the Minas) shows wealth and riches in action. The master gave his servants a lump sum: that was a type of inheritance. Those servants were handed large sums of money to manage well. After the wealth transfer, the master then expected his servants to "do business till I come" and increase the inheritance. Their ability to increase qualified them for promotion to greater things. Their inability to increase what they'd been given qualified them to have no more opportunities. The increase they created with the inheritance was "riches."

Work the field you've been given (the field itself is a form of wealth – an inheritance), and create more riches through what's been cultivated with your own hands in that field. Wealth and riches are two sides of the same coin.

Start to learn and understand that you're worthy of a good inheritance (gifts, opportunities, referrals, favor). God has inheritances set up for His kids, both here on Earth and in Heaven. Learn to recognize when a blessing has been placed in your lap; that's an inheritance, a gift.

Also learn to steward well the gifts, fields, money, opportunities, and favor you've been given, then increase them to abundance. We take our inheritances and work them, creating riches.

> *"The lines have fallen to me in pleasant places;*
> *Yes, I have a good inheritance."* —Psalm 16:6

Here's something else to consider: in order to receive an inheritance, honor fathers. "Fathers" and "mothers" are people in our lives like mentors, teachers, pastors, coaches, those who have gone before us on a journey, grandparents, and our actual parents. They hold keys to inheritances and desire to pass those keys on to us when we are ready. Mutual honor, even with peers, opens doors.

God's heart for us:
- God wants us to become skilled at working with the inheritances He provides.
- God places inheritances in our hands in order to grow and create riches from them.

CHAPTER 15

THE SECRET TO LIFE MORE ABUNDANTLY

Spiritual Principle: *All abundance stems from a close, personal relationship with the Lord.*

One more time, I'd like to highlight Jesus' powerful statement found in John 10:10. There is a secret found within it:

"I have come that they may have life, and that they may have it more abundantly."

Have you ever wondered why Jesus has two parts to what He says here? By Him coming to Earth, sacrificing Himself to pay the price for our salvation and reconciliation to God, all of humanity was given a special offer, actually...two offers.

1. Life (salvation, Heaven, entrance into His Kingdom, sealed with the Holy Spirit)

2. More Abundant Life (true riches, deep wisdom and revelation, greater spiritual power and authority)

I believe when Jesus talks about being trustworthy with true riches, He means things, resources, information, power, and greater works only available through Him in the Kingdom of God.

"...if you have not been faithful in the unrighteous mammon, who will commit to your trust the true riches?"
— Luke 16:11

Living a clean, godly life according to God's Word and ways is important. Having a heart that cares about what God cares about sets us up for favor. Being a person who doesn't participate with sin or darkness makes life go smoother and keeps our hearts healthy. Things like being faithful to your spouse, trusting God with your money by tithing, having integrity with your words and actions, and being a loving, kind person are all highly valuable.

But there is more than just living a good, Christian life.

All of these godly-living characteristics can set us up for a good life. We can reach a certain place, get to a certain point by doing so, and that place is actually pretty good. Trust me though, even when you reach the good place, there's a sense that there's still so much more. I believe that small seed of dissatisfaction comes from the Lord. He doesn't want us to stay comfy and satisfied with His blessings and the life we've created by living according to His wisdom (even though He is pleased by this); He wants us to desire Him above all, waiting daily at His gates, getting to know Him, becoming like Him.

Here's how we access the abundant level:

Life more abundantly can only be found through a close, deep, intimate relationship with the Lord.

Life more abundantly is the second offer Jesus has for us. Jesus is abundant life, and abundance unfolds as we know Him at deeper levels. All of these things and more are included:

- Spiritual insights and ability more abundantly
- Finances more abundantly
- Vision and creativity more abundantly
- Relationships with others more abundantly

If you've ever desired the greater gifts of the Spirit, if you've ever felt stuck at a certain level in life, if you know there is more, but can't seem to access it, relationship is the secret; it is the answer. The deeper you go, more is unlocked to you.

Think about it. When you are in close relationship with a person, you get access to things and opportunities others do not. For example, because my dad was a teacher at the elementary school I attended, I had access to the teacher's lounge. Other kids did not. When my sister was the worship pastor of a large church, I was often invited to sing for special occasions and events. I once had an upcoming class for authors, and a good friend interviewed me about it in her Facebook group. When Chris travels for work, I've had the chance to go with him and see some amazing places around the world.

Imagine how much more this is true with God. A close, daily relationship with God produces abundance. The closer we are with Him, the more abundance we step into – in every area of life (going from glory to glory).

If you are a believer in Jesus, there's no doubt you already have a relationship with the Lord at some level. Maybe you're at the "life" level of salvation, having entered the Kingdom, or maybe you're well beyond that initial step and have been for some time. Maybe you're already an expert at living a godly lifestyle, but abundance and true riches in some areas of life still seems elusive.

There's good news! You are going in the right direction. Wherever you're at today, there is more...a lot more, and it's available to you through an ever-deepening relationship with Jesus.

God's heart for us:
- Abundant life and true riches are found through close, personal relationship with God.
- God longs for us to be closer to Him. Being in relationship with Him brings great reward in every way.

CONCLUSION

What are our belief systems about money? Do our core beliefs and mindset match God's on this topic? Being on the same page with God when it comes to money is the best financial position to be in. Hopefully as you've read this book, you can now recognize there's a blessing and multiplication that comes with handling money God's way.

This book along with our *Make Your Money Work for You: Level Up Your Finances with New Mindsets, Planning, Habits and Goals* are the two most impactful books in this series. Saving money is great. Learning how to stretch a dollar is wonderful. Bringing more money into your household's monthly budget is necessary. Investing and planning for your financial future will save you heartache. But without learning and understanding the *Spiritual Principles of Money* and having the right mindset, your financial growth may still suffer. Either it will stay small, matching small thinking, or the weight of having money may turn you into someone who you don't like when you look in the mirror.

Here at Save Money and Build Wealth, our team would like to encourage you to continue learning God's principles for every area of life. Like money, there is wisdom for our relationships, health and well-being, families, work, and every aspect of life found in the

Bible. Through *The Abundance Plan Book Series*, coaching, our Facebook group and workshop opportunities, we want to continue coaching you on money mindset, stewardship and increase.

By the way, if you're new to Bible reading and don't know where to start, visit www.BibleGateway.com and type in a specific keyword, topic or phrase you're interested in learning more about. Some people simply start reading the Bible at the beginning in Genesis, although you don't have to. We recommend starting out by reading Proverbs or John.

In order to grow and steward our money well, in order to save money and build wealth, we need God's wisdom and help. He is the smartest, wisest person for every aspect of life! His paths drip with abundance and have peace built into them. We encourage you to read through these *Spiritual Principles of Money* as many times as you need to and share them with others.

At Save Money and Build Wealth, our team is praying for your financial breakthrough, which will start first within you – in your heart and mindset!

Many blessings,
Krista Dunk

PRAYER

If you have the desire to know more about God and live your life according to His plans, ask Him for help. That may seem odd and unfamiliar – talking to an unseen person. Maybe you've never "prayed" before, but that's where we all start...at the beginning. Many of us have started with, "God, if You're real, show me. If You're there, I want to know You more." Or, some of us have started a relationship with God out of desperation. "God, please help me!"

He hears every thought you have and every unspoken request. He has been there, every day of your life, wanting you to choose to have a relationship with Him. If you are sincere in your desire to know Him, He will reveal Himself to you. He's been waiting. A simple prayer like this (or however you want to say it) can start your journey with the Lord:

God, thank you for hearing me. You know me better than I know myself. I believe You sent Jesus to pay the price for my sin by dying on the cross and raising to life again. I believe, Jesus' blood shed for me gives me access to Your Kingdom now. Help any areas of unbelief I may still have. Forgive all my sins. I want to know You more. Teach me Your ways. Reveal Yourself to me. Help me understand how to live an abundant life. Because I have accepted Jesus, I am made right in Your eyes. Bless me Lord, and help me to be a blessing to others.
In Jesus' name I pray, amen.

"For God so loved the world that He gave His only begotten Son, that whoever believes in Him should not perish but have everlasting life." —John 3:16

"If you confess with your mouth the Lord Jesus and believe in your heart that God has raised Him from the dead, you will be saved. For with the heart one believes unto righteousness, and with the mouth confession is made unto salvation." —Romans 10:9-10

Recommended Resources

Money Mysteries from the Master, By Gary Keesee
How Heaven Invades Your Finances, by Jim Baker
Poverty, Riches & Wealth, by Kris Vallotton
Business Prosperity and Training: **100X Academy**
Miracles and Healing: **www.SidRoth.org**
It's Supernatural TV and radio show: **www.SidRoth.org**
Online Bible Reading and Research:
www.BibleGateway.com
Inspirational Radio: **www.Air1.com**

"Wisdom is good with an inheritance…"
— Ecclesiastes 7:11a

"Why do you spend money for what is not bread, and your wages for what does not satisfy? Listen carefully to Me, and eat what is good, and let your soul delight itself in abundance." — Isaiah 55:2

Save Money & Build Wealth

The Abundance Plan

Connect with us more:

Website:
www.SaveMoneyandBuildWealth.com

Facebook:
www.facebook.com/groups/savemoneyandbuildwealth

Instagram:
@savemoneyandbuildwealth, @krista.dunk

Pinterest:
www.pinterest.com/kristadunkWA/save-money-and-build-wealth/

TheAbundancePlan@gmail.com

About the Author

Krista Dunk is an author, speaker, real estate investor, and the project director for two book publishing companies. Krista has written several books.

Her first book, *Step Out and Take Your Place*, published in 2011, helps people of God discover their God-given gifts and calling by taking a journey to seek Him. She has also published a devotional, the Ninja Kitty children's book series, as well as books in The Abundance Plan book series.

As a child and young adult who struggled with timidity, Krista now finds herself speaking and training in front of audiences large and small. She is passionate about helping people get a vision for how their life could look and to step out into it.

Krista and Chris, her husband of 26+ years, live in Washington State with their two teenagers. Krista, Chris and their friend, Chris Creekpaum, make up the Save Money and Build Wealth training team.

Learn more at:
www.KristaDunk.com
www.SaveMoneyandBuildWealth.com

Speaking and Training

Interested in speakers for your group, event, conference, church, or online training on faith and finance topics? Looking to host a special workshop or need small group curriculum to help people save money and build wealth?

Connect with the Save Money and Build Wealth team today – Chris, Krista and Chris! This power trio is fun, experienced and loves to help others get breakthrough in the area of money and finances. They are also dedicated to helping people get new, biblically-based mindsets that will give them freedom in many areas of their lives.

Money-Related Training Topic Examples:
101 Ways to Make More Money
101 Ways to Stretch a Dollar
The 5 Uses of Money
Financial Goal Setting
Teen and Young Adult Money Success Kickstart
Stewarding Money God's Way
Money Mindset for Abundance
Discovering Your Money Journey's Next Step

Connect with our team today at
TheAbundancePlan@gmail.com
or on our Facebook group page at
www.facebook.com/groups/savemoneyandbuildwealth

The Abundance Plan Book Series:
Available Now:

<u>Coming soon:</u>
Save Money by DIY'ing Just About Anything
101 Ways to Stretch a Dollar
101 Side Hustles to Make More Money

Exclusive Publishing for Kingdom Entrepreneurs
www.100Xacademy.com